GW00367924

THIS IS A CARLTON BOOK

The Dog Logo and Photographs © 2005
Artlist International Inc
Text and Design copyright © 2004
Carlton Books Limited

This edition published in 2005 by
Carlton Books Ltd
A Division of the Carlton Publishing Group
20 Mortimer Street
London
W1T 3JW

A CIP catalogue for this book is available
from the British Library.

ISBN 1 84442 697 1

Project Editor: Amie McKee
Art Director: Clare Baggaley
Design: Stuart Smith
Production: Caroline Alberti

Printed and bound in Singapore

THE DOG

Artlist Collection

BIG DOGS

CARLTON
BOOKS

German Shepherd

German Shepherd

German Shepherd

Weimaraner

Weimaraner

Akita

Akita

Labrador Retriever

Labrador Retriever

Boxer

Border Collie

Border Collie

Siberian Husky

Siberian Husky

Bloodhound

Doberman

Doberman

Rottweiler

Rottweiler

Golden Retriever

Golden Retriever

Collie

Newfoundland

Irish Setter

Great Pyrénées

Great Pyrénées

Great Pyrénées

Dalmatian

Dalmatian

Saint Bernard

Afghan Hound

Saluki

Bernese Mountain Dog

Bernese Mountain Dog

Samoyed

Poodle

Beauceron

Italian Greyhound

Borzoi

Borzoi

Bearded Collie

Old English Sheepdog

Tosa

Tosa